19.75

W9-ATR-950

DATE DUE

Sir Walter Raleigh

and the Search for El Dorado

Explorers of New Worlds

Sir Walter Raleigh
and the Search for El Dorado

Neil Chippendale

Chelsea House Publishers
Philadelphia

Prepared for Chelsea House Publishers by:
OTTN Publishing, Stockton, N.J.

CHELSEA HOUSE PUBLISHERS
Editor in Chief: Sally Cheney
Associate Editor in Chief: Kim Shinners
Production Manager: Pamela Loos
Art Director: Sara Davis
Director of Photography: Judy L. Hasday
Project Editors: LeeAnne Gelletly, Brian Baughan
Series Designer: Keith Trego

First Printing
1 3 5 7 9 8 6 4 2

Library of Congress Cataloging-in-Publication Data

Chippendale, Neil.
    Sir Walter Raleigh and the search for El
    Dorado / Neil Chippendale.
        p. cm. – (Explorers of new worlds)
Includes bibliographical references and index.
ISBN 0-7910-6434-4 (hardcover : alk. paper) –
1. Raleigh, Walter, Sir, 1552?–1618–Juvenile literature.
2. Great Britain–Court and courtiers–Biography–
Juvenile literature. 3. America–Discovery and
exploration–Juvenile literature. 4. Explorers–England–
Biography–Juvenile literature. 5. El Dorado–Juvenile
literature. [1. Raleigh, Walter, Sir, 1552?–1618.
2. Explorers.] I. Title. II. Series.

DA86.22.R2 C48 2001
942.055'092–dc21
[B]   2001028270

Contents

The Lost Colony

W A

I

A

P E

C Ehesepiooc

Skicoak

Chesepiooc sinus

Come

Apasus

OCCIDENS

SEPTENTRIO

A 16th-century map of Virginia, based on watercolor paintings by John White. Between 1578 and 1590, Sir Walter Raleigh organized several attempts to colonize Virginia, but none succeeded. Perhaps the most famous of these is the "lost" colony at Roanoke Island.

I

A s the English ship *Hopewell* slowly approached the wooded shores of the Outer Banks opposite Roanoke Island on August 17, 1590, Captain Abraham Cocke fired a cannon to announce the arrival of the ship carrying governor John White. On that island three years earlier, acting on behalf of Sir Walter Raleigh, White had established what was meant to be the first permanent English colony in North America.

In 1587 Raleigh had sent out a group of colonists, ordering them to settle at the Chesapeake Bay, about 80 miles north of Roanoke Island. On the way, the colonists had stopped at the island to pick up 15 men who had been left at another colony the year before. They found only the bones of one of the men. The others had disappeared. The island's fort was a ruin, and all the houses had collapsed.

The worried colonists were eager to get on to the Chesapeake. However, the fleet commander was more interested in raiding Spanish shipping in the Caribbean Sea. He refused to go any farther. All the colonists, and the few supplies they had, were dropped at Roanoke Island.

The most commonly used form of Sir Walter's last name is "Raleigh" and it is the form used in this book. During his lifetime Raleigh spelled his name a variety of ways, but during the last 30 years of his life he often spelled it "Ralegh."

With food running low, White was urged by the settlers to return to England so he could buy supplies for the colony. He planned to return the next year. Unfortunately for the colonists, it took White three years to return.

As the *Hopewell* neared Roanoke, John White must

have been anxious to see the settlers. Among them were White's daughter Elenora, his son-in-law Ananias Dare, and their daughter Virginia Dare, born shortly after their arrival on Roanoke Island. Virginia was the first English child born in America. White probably thought that his arrival would be a cause for joy among the long-abandoned settlers.

The *Hopewell's* crew had seen smoke rising from the island and assumed it came from a fire maintained by the Roanoke colonists. As the sailors rowed White to the island, they blew trumpets, sang English songs, and shouted to get the attention of those left behind in 1587. However, when the men went ashore at the northern tip of the island, White and the sailors found the settlement deserted. The smoke came from an unattended brush fire.

Where had the settlers gone? The only clues came from carvings on two trees in the settlement. On one was carved the letters CROATOAN and on the other CRO. Both probably referred to an island 50 miles south of Roanoke. It was known to be inhabited by Native Americans ruled by Manteo, a friend of White's. White wanted to sail there immediately, but Captain Cocke refused. The weather was turning bad and the ***anchorage*** was not safe for

Puzzled English sailors examine the word "Croatoan" carved onto a tree on Roanoke Island. No one has yet figured out the mystery of what happened to the settlers from the "lost colony."

his ship and its sister ship, the *Moonlight*. Both of the English captains were eager to head for Spanish territory in the Caribbean to raid merchant ships there. The 117 men, women, and children left on Roanoke Island were never seen again.

The fate of the "Lost Colony" has remained a mystery and the subject of many books and stories. Many people believe that the settlers were absorbed into the Croatoan band of Indians. Long afterward reports circulated of blue-eyed Hatteras Indians and of Indians claiming to have white ancestors.

Another theory is that some of the colonists reached the Chesapeake Bay area and were killed by the Indian chief Powhatan around 1607. Perhaps some tried to sail away in a small boat and were lost at sea. A combination of all of these theories could also be true.

Whatever their fate, these colonists made a lasting impression upon American literature and folklore. And their sponsor, Sir Walter Raleigh, had turned England's attention to the distant shores of North America.

A portrait of Sir Walter Raleigh on the deck of a ship. During his lifetime Raleigh led several expeditions to North and South America, and he organized and funded other efforts to colonize and explore the New World.

The English Venture Forth 2

England is located on a large island northwest of Europe. At the time of Christopher Columbus, near the end of the 15th century, English sailors were more interested in fishing than exploring. However, the West Country of England, the island's southwestern *peninsula*, enjoyed a prosperous trade with Iceland and the Azores Islands, off the coast of Portugal. The West Country was nearly surrounded by water, with the English Channel to its south and the Irish Sea to its north. Its busy ports of Plymouth and Bristol soon spawned a new breed of English sailor: those who were eager to explore the world.

Bristol became the home of an Italian sailor named Giovanni Caboto, also known as John Cabot. In 1497, only five years after Columbus sailed to America, Cabot launched his little English ship *Matthew* with a crew of 18 men. The explorers left Bristol's harbor and sailed west looking for an ocean passage to India, referred to as the Northwest Passage. This route would help merchants avoid taking the Spanish and Portuguese trade routes to the **Orient**, and give England its own access to the rich trade with India and China.

After about a month at sea, Cabot and his men found the island of Newfoundland, which is part of present-day Canada. They also found a great number of fish in the waters off the island. Cabot then sailed down the coast of North America, looking for the Northwest Passage. He found no such western route. But before returning to Bristol, Cabot claimed this vast territory for the English king, Henry VII.

The next year Cabot returned with five ships. He planned to make detailed charts of the area. Little is known about this voyage except that Cabot and four of the ships were lost with all hands.

The rich cod-fishing grounds off eastern Canada found by Cabot soon provided a prosperous living for West Country captains. England's first attempt at exploration had netted them a land of rocks, trees, and codfish.

The next voyage by English explorers was an attempt to find a northeast passage to the Orient by sailing around the North Cape of Norway. Two English adventurers, Hugh Willoughby and Richard Chancellor, sailed around Norway and entered the White Sea in 1553-54. Willoughby froze to death, but Chancellor pressed on and landed in Northern Russia. After finding his way to the court of Ivan the Terrible, the ruler of Russia, Chancellor returned to England. He then founded the Muscovy Company to trade with Russia. While Chancellor did not get to China, his trade with Russia through its northern port of Archangel proved very prosperous.

Spain had already explored and established colonies in the New World, mostly in Central America. In 1562, the Plymouth merchant John Hawkins entered the Spanish slave trade. Three times he sailed to West Africa, where he picked up large cargoes of African slaves, then carried them to the Spanish colonies in Central America. Hawkins sold these slaves and returned home with a fortune in Spanish ***doubloons***.

This painting by the 19th century English artist John Everett Millais is titled The Boyhood of Raleigh. *Raleigh was born in an area of England with a rich seafaring tradition; he probably heard many stories as a child that inspired his later travels and adventures.*

The slave trade was not the only way the English got their hands on Spanish gold. The English also attacked Spanish vessels carrying gold and silver from the mines in South America. When the small, quick English ships attacked the large, slow Spanish *galleons*, the English boasted their sailors were as fast and fierce as a dog stealing a bone. They soon began calling themselves "sea dogs." To the Spanish, the English were nothing more than pirates.

On the last of his voyages Hawkins's fleet was attacked by the Spanish and almost destroyed. Hawkins managed to escape and soon returned to England to retire with his wealth. Later, as one of Queen Elizabeth's naval advisors, Hawkins urged the queen to found colonies in North America. He thought these colonies could serve as bases to attack the Spanish.

One of England's most famous and outspoken supporters of colonies in the New World would arrive at the queen's court later in the 16th century: Sir Walter Raleigh.

Born in Devon in the West Country about 1554, Raleigh was the youngest son of minor *gentry*, or small landholders. Although his family name was ancient, the Raleighs were not nobility. They were also penniless. From his youth, Raleigh's goal in life was to enrich himself and improve his social standing. His father sent him to Oxford University, where Raleigh learned quickly and easily. He soon established a reputation for being intelligent and

> **Despite his travels, Raleigh never lost the accent of his childhood. As someone once said, he "spake broad Devonshire until his dying day."**

gifted. After spending some time in France, Raleigh returned to England to study law in London.

Raleigh was not just an intellectual. He began a life of action in his youth. As a teenager he fought with the Huguenot ***Protestants*** in France, and he saw naval action with his elder half-brother, Sir Humphrey Gilbert. Unfortunately, he also earned a reputation for having a bad temper. Twice he had short stays in prison for brawling. As a young man, Raleigh was clearly more ready for adventure than for further study.

Early in his twenties, Raleigh received both an opportunity for adventure and his first taste of the New World. A small group of men from Raleigh's home county of Devon were advancing the idea of English colonization of the new lands in America. Sir Humphrey Gilbert, Raleigh himself, and their cousin Sir Richard Grenville were the leaders of this group. Gilbert wanted to find the Northwest Passage around America to the Orient, which England had been seeking for nearly a century. Gilbert also thought that England's path to being a great power depended on starting English colonies in the New World. In 1578, Gilbert got a ***patent***, or contract, from Queen Elizabeth authorizing the settlement of North America in any areas not presently occupied by any Christian ruler.

However, most of Gilbert's ships sent to colonize America in 1578 never even left English waters. They were turned back by bad weather and storms. The ship *Falcon*, captained by Raleigh, attempted to sail on to the West Indies in the Caribbean to raid the Spanish treasure ships. He too met with failure,

Sir Richard Grenville, Raleigh's cousin, was a partner in a 1578 attempt to establish English colonies in North America. However, the expedition failed to even reach North America. In 1585, Grenville would lead a much larger expedition to Virginia, sponsored by Raleigh.

Sir Humphrey Gilbert was about 17 years older than his half-brother, Walter Raleigh. In 1583 he established an English colony at St. John's, Newfoundland; however, Gilbert drowned when his ship sank on the homeward journey.

returning with a battered and bruised ship and no treasure.

After spending several years raising money for exploration and colonization, Gilbert set out again in 1583 with five ships and 260 men. Again, one of the ships was owned and captained by Raleigh. The men Gilbert had recruited for his colony included **masons**, or stoneworkers; carpenters who would work with wood; smiths who would forge iron tools and weapons; and "mineral men and refiners," who would mine the gold he hoped to find. During the voyage across the Atlantic, the men on Raleigh's ship became very sick with **dysentery**. He chose to return to England.

Gilbert pressed on with his remaining ships and landed at Newfoundland. While the ship *William* went cod fishing, the men on the remaining three ships looked for "savages" and a good place for a settlement. They stopped to establish a colony at St. John's, Newfoundland; however, Gilbert thought that both Newfoundland and the mainland area, called Labrador, were too cold and barren for a successful colony.

Gilbert's fleet then sailed south looking for warmer shores. The largest ship in the fleet, *Delight,* ran aground off Nova Scotia and was destroyed along with most of the expedition's supplies. After much discussion the remaining ships turned around and headed back to England. Unfortunately for Gilbert, his small ship, the *Squirrel,* was lost at sea near the Azores, and Gilbert drowned.

The expedition had been doomed from the start by poor leadership and bad planning. Raleigh learned many lessons from his half-brother's failure.

The long reign of Queen Elizabeth, from 1558 to 1603, coincided with the emergence of England as a political and cultural world power. Walter Raleigh became a favorite at the queen's court between 1581 and 1592.

Raleigh, Ireland, and Queen Elizabeth

3

aleigh's early adventures were not limited to voyages to the New World. He was also involved in warfare and politics in Ireland. When the ruling position of Munster, an Irish **province**, became vacant, Gilbert, Raleigh, Grenville, and others from the West Country of England supported the claim of Sir Peter Carew to rule the old kingdom of Cork, which was a part of Munster. By supporting Carew, Gilbert and Raleigh were able to increase their wealth.

Some people in Munster fought back during the Desmond Rebellion of 1569-73. Gilbert and Raleigh suppressed these rebels with harshness and cruelty. Their actions resulted in the merciless slaughter of many Irish. The Englishmen succeeded in ending the rebellion, however, and Humphrey Gilbert was knighted by the queen.

Queen Elizabeth wanted to bring English law to Ireland. This law would include recognizing Elizabeth as the head of the church. Because the Church of England was Protestant and the Irish people were Catholic, this was bound to cause trouble. The English law also took away the local rulers' power to tax their residents. The native Irish nobility did not like losing their tax money and were constantly in revolt.

Many of the Irish hoped the Catholic king Philip II of Spain would invade their country and drive out the English. Philip, however proved to be a disappointing *patron*. During Philip's long reign he was kept busy dealing with revolt in the Spanish-ruled Protestant Netherlands and with maintaining Spain's empire in Europe and the New World. Only when England began helping the Dutch with their revolt did Philip seriously help the Irish rebels.

In 1580, Philip and the Catholic pope in Rome sent 700 Spanish and Italian soldiers to help Ireland.

Rather than move about the country, the soldiers built a fort at Smerwick, in the south of Ireland. The English reacted very quickly to the landing and attacked the troops before the local Irish rebels could come to their aid. The English ruler of Ireland, Lord Deputy Grey de Wilton, and Raleigh besieged the fort and forced the town to surrender. In Wilton's view the Spanish soldiers were no more than pirates, and he ordered them to be killed. Whether Raleigh supported this massacre is not known, but he did not criticize it. The warfare in Ireland was noted for its brutality, but at the time, the English believed such cruelty was necessary.

Raleigh's adventures in Ireland earned him a reputation as a brave soldier and a resourceful commander. As a reward, the queen *confiscated* land in Ireland, some of which she gave to Raleigh. This was part of Elizabeth's plan to replace local Irish lords with Englishmen loyal to her. Many Englishmen wanted to establish colonies or "plantations" in the fertile areas of Ireland.

When Walter Raleigh returned from Ireland in 1581, he headed for the center of power in England: the court of Queen Elizabeth. Elizabeth's reign marked the flowering of the English Renaissance.

Fashion, poetry, and other elements of high culture were very popular among the wealthy, including the queen herself. She liked to have men around her who were adventurous, suave, and intelligent. Sir Walter Raleigh fit that description and soon caught the queen's eye.

Very handsome and standing over six feet tall, with dark hair and a trim beard, Raleigh impressed the ladies. To be noticed, he dressed in bright colors and flashing jewelry. The revenue from his Irish lands gave Raleigh the money he needed to pay for his rich clothes, fine jewelry, and grand houses. Having no wife to divert him from his devotion to the queen, he wrote love ***sonnets*** and often tried to impress her. Reports of his ***gallantry*** became legend.

In the most famous account, Raleigh gained the queen's favor by throwing

The queen occasionally indulged in romances with her favorites; in addition to Raleigh, she had affairs with Robert Dudley, the Earl of Leicester, and later with Robert Devereux, the Earl of Essex, until his rebelliousness led to his execution in 1601. However, Queen Elizabeth never married. She was known as the "Virgin Queen" for this reason.

This engraving from a 17th century book depicts the most famous story about Sir Walter Raleigh. The nobleman spreads his cloak before Queen Elizabeth, so the queen will not get her feet dirty in a mud puddle.

his cloak over a puddle to prevent her feet from getting wet. Another legend had Raleigh exchanging poetic lines with the queen by scratching them on a windowpane with his diamond ring. Elizabeth seemed genuinely captivated by this man, who was young enough to be her son. In 1587, Raleigh was made the captain of the queen's guard.

Yet, as much as Elizabeth liked him, he never became one of her close advisors. Still, Raleigh would benefit greatly from the queen's affection. To help Raleigh, the queen issued a number of letters of patent to him from which he might gain income.

Elizabethan Poetry

Poetry was an important part of the court of Elizabeth. The queen's admirers flattered her with adoring poems and ballads. Raleigh was the author of many poems. His poetry was dedicated to the queen, and was often about his love for her. This poem by Raleigh can be read either across or down:

Hir face	Hir tongue	Hir wit
So faire	So sweete	So sharpe
First bent	Then drew	Then hit
Mine eie	Mine eare	My heart
Mine eie	Mine eare	My heart
To like	To learne	To love
Her face	Hir tong	Hir wit
Doth lead	Doth teach	Doth move
Oh face	Oh tong	Oh wit
With frownes	With cheeke	With smarte
Wrong not	Vex not	Wound not
Mine eie	Mine eare	My heart
Mine eie	Mine eare	My heart
To learne	To knowe	To feare
Hir face	Hir tong	Hir wit
Doth lead	Doth teach	Doth sweare

Raleigh's most famous sonnet was titled "Methought I saw the grave where Laura Lay." It appears in the introduction to a long poem by Edmund Spenser called *The Faerie Queen*. Raleigh helped to get Spenser's book published; it is considered one of the most important poems of the Elizabethan age.

One of the queen's powers was to make grants for the regulation of trade. The queen's government gave ***monopoly*** rights to individuals by issuing them letters of patent. These rights of patent took many forms. In one a person might be licensed to do things not otherwise allowed by English law. In another a person might be permitted to export goods that others were forbidden to sell. People were also given the right to issue licenses to others.

In 1588 Sir Walter Raleigh obtained the patent to issue licenses to taverns. Raleigh was also given control over the sale of playing cards. In addition, Raleigh sent ships, called ***privateers***, to attack the Spanish ships in the Caribbean and take their gold and silver. His sponsorship of these English privateers meant the Spanish considered Raleigh one of the hated sea dogs.

The most important patent Raleigh received had to do with the New World. After he learned of his half brother's death at sea, Raleigh went to the queen to ask permission to continue the colonizing efforts. Within six months of the death of Sir Humphrey Gilbert, Queen Elizabeth granted Raleigh's request for the patent to colonize North America.

SECOTAN

Pasquenc

Dasamongueptic

Roanoac

Trinety harbor

Hatorasck

Explorers of New Worlds

Raleigh's
Colony and
the Spanish

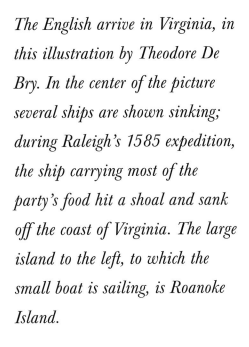

The English arrive in Virginia, in this illustration by Theodore De Bry. In the center of the picture several ships are shown sinking; during Raleigh's 1585 expedition, the ship carrying most of the party's food hit a shoal and sank off the coast of Virginia. The large island to the left, to which the small boat is sailing, is Roanoke Island.

4

he patent from Queen Elizabeth gave Raleigh permission to set up colonies in any part of North America not occupied by any other Christian power. But although the queen supported Raleigh's colonization efforts, she would not let him go exploring or colonizing himself. She wished to keep him at court with her. The queen did not want anything to happen to her favorite. Raleigh would have to explore through others.

He quickly sent out two ships on a mission to explore the east coast of North America to find a suitable place for a colony. These ships, under Philip Amadas and Arthur Barlowe, followed the usual route to the Caribbean Sea and then sailed north. Amadas landed in islands off the North Carolina coast. He established contact with some Native Americans who were uncommonly friendly, and the English sailors spent a few pleasant weeks on Roanoke Island. Confident that they had found an earthly paradise, Amadas and Barlowe returned to England, bringing with them two Native Americans.

Another person on this same voyage was John White. Raleigh sent him to Roanoke Island as the expedition's artist and mapmaker. He came back with a set of watercolor paintings that became a primary source for the study of the plants, animals, and people native to this part of North America.

Needing money for a real colonizing venture, Raleigh hoped to win financial support from Queen Elizabeth and others. To promote the idea of colonization, Raleigh enlisted the help of his friend Richard Hakluyt. Hakluyt was a young minister who had served as chaplain and secretary to the queen's ambassador in Paris. While in France, he had spoken with many of the French explorers of the New World, and he believed that England deserved a share of North America. Hakluyt explained his views to Queen Elizabeth. He also published several **pamphlets** on the subject. Soon the queen and her advisers agreed that creating colonies was the proper goal of exploration. North American colonies would allow England to appear as successful as Holland, France, Portugal, and Spain. An English colony in America could also serve as a base for attacks against the Spanish. These attacks would bring home valuable cargoes of wine, olive oil, gold, and silver.

Amadas and Barlowe's reports of friendly natives and good soil on the east coast of America, near Roanoke Island, were also used to promote a new colony. The two Native Americans they had brought back to England, Manteo and Wanchese, became very popular with the wealthy people of London. Manteo and Wanchese also taught Raleigh's men their language and promised to help the English when they returned to America.

The two Native Americans, John White's book of painting and maps, and the expedition's report were presented to Queen Elizabeth. She was very pleased. Raleigh received permission from her to name these new lands Virginia in her honor as the unmarried Virgin Queen of England. Early in 1585 the queen knighted Raleigh and named him "Lord and Governor of Virginia." However, the queen was worried about provoking Spain and did not directly support Raleigh's colonization plan.

Raleigh's roles as the queen's favorite **courtier** and the captain of her personal guard did not allow him to accompany the expedition to America. His friend and cousin, Sir Richard Grenville, was given command of the ships. A soldier, Ralph Lane, would command the colonists once they arrived at Roanoke. A friend of Raleigh's, Thomas Harriot, went along to serve as the chief scientist and to work with the Native Americans. Harriot was a brilliant young scientist from Oxford who taught **navigation** to some of Raleigh's sailors. Raleigh himself had attended these classes, probably remembering his brother Sir Humphrey Gilbert's fate at sea.

In April 1585 six ships, carrying 500 sailors and 100 colonists, left Plymouth Harbor to sail to North America. Unfortunately, this first settlement was not a success. When the colonists first arrived, the ship carrying most of their **provisions** struck a shoal and

This illustration of Native Americans fishing in Virginia was made from paintings by John White, a member of one of Raleigh's colonizing expeditions.

sank as it approached Roanoke Island. It was too late in the season to plant crops, and the settlers had to trade with the natives for food to survive. The colonists could not find any gold or silver. The only things that seemed to be of interest were the native tobacco and black pearls found in the bay.

These colonists were soldiers, not settlers. They expected to be supplied by the local natives and an annual delivery by ships from home. However, the local Native Americans, who had been so friendly during Amadas's earlier visit, had hardly enough food for themselves. During the harsh and stormy winter they had nothing to spare for the settlers. These Indians also lost their awe of the visitors as the English soldiers showed themselves to be ordinary people, not gods. In addition, the Native Americans were not happy that the settlers intended to be their permanent neighbors. The Indians soon became unfriendly toward the Englishmen.

The colonists' leader, Ralph Lane, had no idea how to establish the colony. When Lane became convinced that the Indians were about to attack, he launched a strike against them instead. This left the colonists isolated, desolate, and hungry. When Grenville did not return with supplies early in 1586, the settlers began to talk of going home.

Luckily, Sir Francis Drake, one of the most famous English sea dogs, arrived on the shores of Roanoke Island. With him was a large fleet of ships from his most recent raid on Spanish ports in the Caribbean. He offered a ship and some provisions

Sir Francis Drake was among the most famous Elizabethan sailors. He was raiding Spanish settlements in the Cape Verde Islands, West Indies, and Central America before stopping to pick up the English colonists at Roanoke Island in 1586.

to tide the **garrison** over until Grenville could return. But a storm threatened the ships in Roanoke's unsafe anchorage and the settlers asked for passage home. Only a few days after Drake, Lane, and the colonists left, Grenville arrived at the colony. He found only three men who had been left behind by mistake. Grenville left 15 soldiers to maintain the English claim to the colony and returned to England himself. The token garrison of 15 men was never seen again.

Raleigh was very disappointed with the failure of the colony, but he did not give up. He obtained additional money from a London company and

sent a new expedition to settle in Virginia in 1587.
Led by John White, this group included men and
women and was designed to distribute land and cre-
ate a true settlement. The colonists included White's
daughter and son-in-law.

White hoped to stop at Roanoke Island, which
he planned to leave under the care of Manteo, the
Indian who had been taken to England in 1584.
After dropping off Manteo, White and the colonists
would then sail on to the Chesapeake Bay, where
White expected to found the new city of Raleigh.
But the ship's master and pilot, Simon Fernandez,
refused to go further than Roanoke Island.

Supplies were scarce, and prospects at Roanoke
Island were bleak. The colonists begged White to
set sail in a small boat to return to England for supplies. White left in August and did not get back to
England until early November. He quickly got help
from Raleigh to outfit a small ship with supplies for
Roanoke. But this small boat never sailed. Neither
did a larger fleet organized by Grenville in the
spring of 1588. The English government refused to
let any ships leave. They would be needed to defend
England from a Spanish attack.

King Philip II of Spain, a Catholic, was now

determined to invade England and remove the Protestant Elizabeth from the throne. The fact that the queen supported privateers such as John Hawkins and Francis Drake—whom the Spanish considered pirates—angered Philip. He could not let the challenges of Drake, Hawkins, Raleigh, and the other sea dogs go unanswered. He also knew that Queen Elizabeth was helping the people of the Netherlands to revolt against Spanish rule. Philip decided that he had to crush Protestant England and return it to the Catholic faith.

Early in 1588, Queen Elizabeth prepared for war. The navy would be the front line of defense, but land forces also had to be organized. England had no army. Instead, each community provided a company of soldiers to fight for the queen. The nobles who ruled each English county organized and equipped these companies. The English nobles also supplied horses and men for a cavalry. By these means, over 50,000 men and 10,000 horses were organized for the defense of England.

Sir Walter Raleigh was appointed a member of the queen's war council and then placed in charge of defending southwest England. It was his duty to organize the soldiers against the expected invasion.

He moved soldiers, cavalry, and equipment to key points along the English coast. If the English fleet failed in its job, Raleigh and his men would have to defeat the Spanish soldiers.

Upon every large hill, Raleigh had baskets of pitch and tar placed on tall poles. They would be lit at the first sight of the Spanish fleet. These 1,000 torches would serve as an early warning system. By this method the message could reach London in less than 20 minutes. A standard messenger on horseback would have taken many hours to travel the same distance.

On July 19, 1588, the first ships of the Spanish Armada were seen approaching England. As the warning torches burst into brilliant flame, people across southern England knew that the battle was about to begin.

The great Spanish Armada contained more than 130 ships. It was commanded by a Spanish noble, the Duke of Medina Sidonia. The Spanish method of warfare called for their ships to pull directly alongside an enemy ship. Then, soldiers would climb from the Spanish vessels to the English ships and fight hand-to-hand with swords and muskets. Medina Sidonia had thousands of soldiers on his

King Philip II of Spain ruled over an empire that included vast territories in Central and South America. In 1588, frustrated with continued attacks by English sea dogs like Francis Drake, Philip ordered an invasion of England. He sent his army to Holland. Once Spain's mighty Armada cleared enemy ships out of the English Channel and seized a port, the army could cross the channel, invade England, and force the queen to submit.

ships ready for this battle. The English however, had smaller, faster ships armed with cannons. Their strategy was to bombard the Spanish fleet from a distance and run away if the Spanish came close.

For several days, the two fleets sailed through the English Channel firing at each other. Neither side could win an advantage.

Although the Spanish Armada contained many ships, the English vessels were faster and better armed. The Spaniards needed to capture a port in England so that they could land troops in the country. The English fleet prevented this, but storms, not sea dogs, eventually destroyed most of the Spanish vessels.

On the evening of July 28, the Spanish fleet anchored at the French port of Calais. The English then launched their secret weapon. Ships filled with explosives and loaded guns were set on fire and sent drifting toward the Spanish fleet. These fire ships frightened the Spanish captains, and they cut their anchor lines and sailed out to sea. There, other English ships were waiting, and they attacked the confused Spaniards without mercy. During the nine-hour Battle of Gravelines, many of the Spanish ships were sunk or badly damaged.

Over the next few days, the remaining Spanish ships sailed northward. When they ran into violent storms, the damaged ships began to sink, and the rest of the fleet was scattered. The Armada was forced to return to Spain by sailing around the British Isles. Medina Sidonia's own ship took a month to return, and it was so banged up it could not be used again.

Philip's great crusade against England had ended in disaster. Not one Spaniard set foot on English soil to challenge Sir Walter Raleigh's soldiers.

Commenting on the failed invasion, Raleigh said, "[T]o invade by sea upon a perilous coast, being neither in possession of any port, nor succored by any party, may better fit a prince presuming on his fortune than enriched with understanding." In other words, Raleigh thought that King Philip had trusted too much to luck. English ships and English sailors had proved their worth, and so had their queen and Sir Walter Raleigh.

Sir Walter Raleigh confers with some of his men during a 1595 expedition to South America. After Raleigh fell out of favor with the queen, he decided to seek redemption—and a fortune—by finding El Dorado, a fabled land of gold.

Disgrace and El Dorado 5

While Spain and England prepared for war, the colonists on Roanoke Island were left on their own. Although he was not allowed to leave England while the Spanish Armada threatened, White finally sailed with two small supply boats with Raleigh's help. However, he was attacked by a French privateer and forced to return to England.

In the early months of 1589, after the danger from the Spanish had passed, Raleigh obtained money from some London merchants to send reinforcements to Roanoke. But nothing happened until the spring of 1590, when

White finally set sail with two privateering vessels that promised to land him at Roanoke. It was on this voyage that he found the colony abandoned.

It is quite possible that the colonists had merely moved into the interior. But, the *Hopewell's* captain, eager to leave, would not let White explore the area to look for his family and the other colonists. The mystery of the Virginia colony has never been solved. White held out hope that the colonists were living on Croatoan Island with Manteo, but he was never able to come back and search for them.

To many people it seemed that Raleigh's attempts at colonization were total failures. The only result seemed to be the abandoned stockade on Roanoke Island. However, Raleigh's efforts set the stage for future colonization attempts. Ralph Lane, the leader of Raleigh's first colony, remembered a great bay to the north that he thought might be a better place for settlers. In addition, Raleigh's friend Richard Hakluyt had created a taste for exotic lands across the sea with the publication of a book about exploration, *Principal Navigations, Voyages and Discoveries of the English Nation,* in 1589.

In 1607 another group of colonists entered the Chesapeake Bay and established a colony called

English settlers work on the fort at Jamestown, the first permanent English settlement in Virginia. Although Raleigh's attempts at colonization failed, his efforts helped to make later attempts, like the colony at Jamestown and others that followed, successful.

Jamestown between the York and James Rivers. This colony was wisely established on a peninsula rather than a sandy island. Jamestown became the first lasting English colony in the New World. Despite their failures, Raleigh, Gilbert, Grenville, Hakluyt, Lane, and White were the founders of the British colonial presence in the New World.

The failed Roanoke colony was not Raleigh's only problem in the early 1590s. In 1592, Raleigh married one of the queen's attendants. He kept the match a secret while continuing to profess devotion to the queen. When Elizabeth found out, Raleigh and his wife, Bess Throckmorton, were imprisoned in the Tower of London in separate apartments. Once banished from court, Raleigh had few friends there to help him.

After two months in the Tower, Raleigh was released to manage a crisis. English captains, financed by Raleigh, had captured a Portuguese merchant ship loaded with tons of pearls, diamonds, silks, and other valuables. The sailors began stuffing their pockets with this treasure, and merchants in the port of Dartmouth were buying the treasure at discount prices. Raleigh was told to stop the *plunder* and protect the queen's profit. Raleigh was able to recover most of the treasure. In thanks, the queen freed Raleigh and his wife. Elizabeth also let him resume his duties as captain of the queen's guard, but he never returned to the queen's favor.

One last Elizabethan enterprise remained for Raleigh: the search for El Dorado, the legendary golden country of South America.

The search for gold had helped drive the exploration of the New World from the beginning. Columbus found some gold in the West Indies, and Hernando Cortés and Francisco Pizarro found more gold as they conquered the Aztecs in Mexico and the Incas in Peru. Yet the Spanish *conquistadors* found no gold mines. This raised the question— where was the source of this precious metal? By the late 16th century, Spanish explorers had narrowed

The El Dorado legend first appeared in the writings of Gonzalo Fernandez de Oviedo in 1541. Oviedo wrote of a chief who covered his naked body daily with fine gold dust. This dust was washed off in a lake each evening. Time and imagination transformed the lake into a city of gold. Soon this city became an entire country of gold. By the time Raleigh arrived in 1595 the location of the fabled land was thought to be somewhere south of the Orinoco River. Today we know that one tribe held an annual ceremony in which a chief's body was covered in gold dust, followed by a ritual washing in a lake. There never was a country of gold.

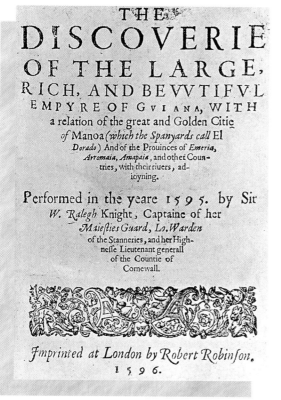

THE
DISCOVERIE
OF THE LARGE,
RICH, AND BEVVTIFVL
EMPYRE OF Gviana, WITH
a relation of the great and Golden Citie
of Manoa (which the Spanyards call El
Dorado) And of the Prouinces of Emeria,
Arromaia, Amapaia, and other Coun-
tries, with their riuers, ad-
ioyning.

Performed in the yeare 1595. by Sir
W. Ralegh Knight, Captaine of her
Maiesties Guard, Lo. Warden
of the Stanneries, and her High-
nesse Lieutenant generall
of the Countie of
Cornewall.

Jmprinted at London by Robert Robinson.
1 5 9 6.

After his failed attempt to find the fabled gold mines of El Dorado in 1595, Raleigh wrote a book about his adventures in Guiana.

its supposed site down to the inaccessible mountains of Guiana. Guiana lies between the basins of the Orinoco and the Amazon Rivers in northeastern South America.

Influenced both by Spanish documents and by stories he'd heard from Native Americans, Raleigh was convinced of the existence of El Dorado. Raleigh also knew about a Spaniard named Domingo de Vera who had traveled up the Caroni River. Vera had reported that two million people lived in the Guiana highlands and wore every variety of gold ornaments. Vera also reported that the capital of El Dorado—Manoa, a city of gold— was only an 11-day trek beyond the furthest point he had reached. Raleigh's imagination was fired by these stories. When his 1592 disgrace at court left him with nothing else to do, he devoted himself to the tasks of exploring Guiana and finding the city of gold.

In 1595 Raleigh sailed to the Caribbean island of Trinidad and established a base. From there he sailed to northeastern South America. The only way into Guiana's mountains seemed to be up a ***tributary*** of the Orinoco River. Every attempt to sail up these tributaries was blocked by huge waterfalls hundreds of feet tall. Raleigh ordered his men to build small boats to voyage upriver. But after four weeks of searching the tributaries Raleigh gave up. He was disgusted with the heat and dirt and worn out by hardships. Raleigh was now nearly 45, and his life at court had not equipped him for this kind of work. Discouraged, he returned to England.

Upon his return Raleigh wrote a book that repeated and blended the El Dorado stories. A little later, Raleigh sent another fleet to investigate the Guiana coast itself for access into the interior, but the ships did not find any inland route.

King James VI of Scotland became James I of England after the death of Queen Elizabeth in 1603. The new king distanced himself from court advisors who had advocated war with Spain. He ordered Raleigh imprisoned in the Tower of London for 13 years.

The End of an Era

6

While Raleigh was in disgrace, an even younger man had emerged as the queen's new favorite at court: Robert Devereux, the Earl of Essex. Tall and handsome, Essex managed to capture the queen's eye.

In 1596, when another war with Spain seemed likely, Essex, Raleigh, Lord Howard of Effingham, and Francis Vere led an expedition that captured the port of Cádiz in Spain. They held it for two weeks. During this time Cádiz was completely plundered and burned. The fleet returned in triumph, but Raleigh was no richer. The expedition had netted little treasure, and Raleigh had not regained his prestige at court. In 1597, the same foursome commanded another fleet sent to raid the Spanish treasure fleet in the Azores Islands. Bad weather and bad leadership allowed the Spanish ships to slip by untouched, and Raleigh and his ships returned empty-handed.

After the success at Cádiz, Essex became one of Elizabeth's most important advisors. In 1598, when Irish rebels again threatened English rule, the queen sent Essex to end the revolt. However, he failed, and this angered Elizabeth. Essex decided to make a desperate attempt to seize power.

Raleigh heard that Essex was plotting to kill the queen and raced to warn the court. Essex and about 300 of his followers were captured in London. After a quick trial, Essex was found guilty of *treason* and executed.

After the death of Essex, the aging Elizabeth often

Raleigh's efforts to stop Essex (pictured here) did not improve his fortunes. With money running low, Raleigh had to sell his lands in Ireland to the Earl of Cork in 1602.

became depressed. In March 1603, at the age of 69, she grew feverish and resigned herself to death. Before she died in the early hours of March 24, Elizabeth named James VI, the king of Scotland, as her successor.

The new king of England, renamed James I, came to the throne at the age of 37. One of his first acts was to seek peace with Spain and end a war that had dragged on for years. Because Raleigh had been an enemy of Spain, he was cast in a bad light toward the king. Raleigh's enemies conspired against him and accused him of treason. In 1603, he was tried, convicted on poor evidence, and sentenced to death. Luckily, King James converted the sentence to life imprisonment.

Raleigh spent the next 13 years in the Tower of London, where he wrote his book *The History of the World*, several poems, and other works that earned him a place among the intellectuals of his time. As a prisoner in the Tower Raleigh was a curiosity, and crowds would watch him take his evening strolls.

Eventually, Raleigh convinced King James to let him return to Guiana to search for the gold of El Dorado. Released on probation in 1616, the 64-year-old Raleigh was instructed by King James not to make any hostile moves against the Spanish while on the quest in South America. Raleigh organized an expedition of 13 ships and 1,000 men to chase his dreams of gold one last time.

Upon reaching the mouth of the Orinoco River, Raleigh discovered a Spanish fort guarding the passage. Too old to take part in any operations, Raleigh stayed back on his ship and sent his men up the Orinoco. One of the leaders of this expedition was Raleigh's son Walter "Wat" Raleigh.

Raleigh's men did not heed their instructions. Instead, they attacked a Spanish village, and Wat Raleigh was killed. The rest of the men made a few futile attempts to find the gold mines and then returned to the fleet. When Raleigh learned of the attack, he realized that the expedition was now a complete disaster. Rejecting the idea of fleeing, Raleigh sailed home in 1618 to face the king. This time he was sentenced to death.

As he faced the executioner, Raleigh managed to keep his humor. Asking to see the executioner's ax he said, "This is a sharp medicine, but it is a sure cure for all diseases." His head was embalmed and presented to his wife, Bess, who kept it until her death 29 years later.

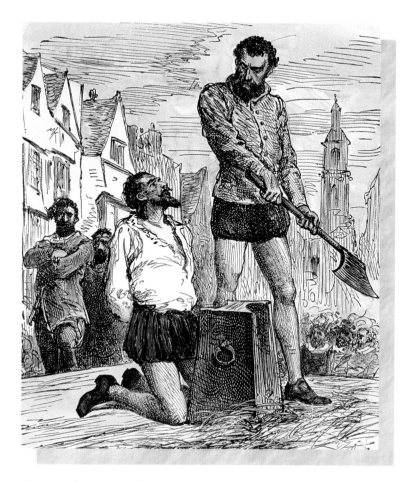

Sir Walter Raleigh faces death at the executioner's block.
Though he died in disgrace, Raleigh remains an
important and fascinating figure of English history.

So ended the life of Sir Walter Raleigh. Active, ambitious, and sometimes quarrelsome, he rose from humble beginnings to the court of Elizabeth I. Sir Walter Raleigh played a leading role in the social, political, and cultural world of his time and earned a place in history.

Chronology

1497 John Cabot explores eastern North America for England.

1554? Walter Raleigh is born in Hayes Barton, Devon.

1562 John Hawkins enters the Spanish slave trade.

1568 Raleigh studies at Oxford University.

1569 Fights with the Huguenots in France.

1575 Returns to England to study law.

1580 Raleigh's elder half brother, Sir Humphrey Gilbert, is given a patent to colonize North America; Raleigh takes part in the Smerwick massacre in Ireland.

1581 Raleigh returns from service in Ireland and becomes a favored courtier of Queen Elizabeth.

1582 Queen Elizabeth grants Raleigh and two others charge of Munster in Ireland.

1583 Raleigh's half brother, Sir Humphrey Gilbert, is lost at sea on his way home from an expedition to Newfoundland.

1584 Raleigh receives a charter from the queen to colonize North America, and organizes his first expedition. His two ships are captained by Philip Amadas and Arthur Barlowe; Raleigh knighted by Queen Elizabeth.

1585 Raleigh's second expedition leaves for North America, led by Sir Richard Grenville; the colony at Roanoke Island fails, and the colonists are taken back to England by Francis Drake the next year.

1587 Raleigh's third expedition to America, led by John White, leaves for Virginia and lands at Roanoke Island.

1588 Receives control of part of Cork and Waterford in Ireland; commands the land forces as the Spanish Armada attacks England unsuccessfully.

1590 The Roanoke colony is found abandoned.

1592 Raleigh secretly marries Bess Throckmorton, one of Queen Elizabeth's attendants; the queen then imprisons them in the Tower of London.

1595 Raleigh goes in search of the mythical El Dorado in Guiana; he later writes a book about his adventures.

1596 Helps capture the Spanish port of Cádiz, along with the Earl of Essex, Lord Howard of Effingham, and Francis Vere.

1602 Raleigh sells his last land holdings in Ireland.

1603 Queen Elizabeth dies; Raleigh is convicted of treason against the new king, James I, and is imprisoned in the Tower of London.

1614 Raleigh publishes *The History of the World.*

1616 Is released from the Tower of London; sent on an expedition to find gold in the Orinoco River area of South America.

1618 Is executed on October 29 by James I after the expedition to the Orinoco River fails.

Glossary

anchorage–an area where vessels can be held in place in the water by dropping an anchor.

confiscate–to take something from its owner by governmental authority.

conquistadors–Spanish soldiers who conquered native peoples in Central and South America in the 16th century.

courtier–a person who is in attendance at a royal court.

doubloon–an old Spanish gold coin.

dysentery–a disease in which patients have severe diarrhea.

gallantry–extremely courteous behavior, directed particularly to women.

galleon–a large, heavy sailing ship used by the Spanish for war or to carry treasure from the New World.

garrison–a military post.

gentry–English middle-class people who hold land but are not considered nobility.

mason–a skilled worker who builds with stone or brick.

monopoly–exclusive rights to sell a certain type of product or service.

navigation–the science of directing the course of a seagoing vessel and of determining its position.

Orient–the area to the east of Europe including China, India, and Malaysia.

pamphlet–an unbound printed publication with no cover, or with a paper cover.

patent–an official document that gives the bearer a right or privilege.

patron–a wealthy or influential person that gives money or other assistance.

peninsula–an area of land surrounded by water on three sides, with the fourth side connected to a larger body of land.

plunder–to take goods by force or theft.

privateer–a privately owned ship given permission by its government to attack enemy ships.

Protestants–members of a religious movement in Europe that broke away from the Roman Catholic church during the 15th and 16th centuries.

province–a region of a country, usually separated from other provinces for geographical or political reasons.

provisions–supplies, especially food and water, that are needed for a trip.

sonnet–a 14-line poem with 10 syllables per line and a specific rhyme scheme.

treason–attempting to overthrow or otherwise betray one's government.

tributary–a stream that flows into a larger river or lake.

Further Reading

Aronson, Marc. *Sir Walter Ralegh and the Quest for El Dorado.* New York: Clarion Books, 2000.

Boyle, Charles, ed. *The European Emergence: Time Frame AD 1500-1600.* Richmond, Va.: Time Life Books Inc., 1989.

Brown, Dale M., ed. *The Search for El Dorado.* Richmond, Va.: Time Life Education, 1994.

Dersin, Denise, ed. *In the Realm of Elizabeth: England, AD 1533-1603.* Alexandria, Va.: Time Life Books, 1998.

Duncan, Alice Smith. *Sir Francis Drake and the Struggle for an Ocean Empire.* New York: Chelsea House Publishers, 1993.

MacCaffrey, Wallace. *Elizabeth I.* London: Edward Arnold, 1993.

Milton, Giles. *Big Chief Elizabeth: The Adventures and Fate of the First English Colonists in America.* New York: Farrar, Straus, and Giroux, 2000.

Morgan, Ted. *Wilderness at Dawn: The Settling of the North American Continent.* New York: Simon and Schuster, 1993.

Thomas, Jane Resh. *Behind the Mask: The Life of Queen Elizabeth I.* New York: Clarion Books, 1998.

Picture Credits

NEIL CHIPPENDALE is a Social Studies teacher at Octorara Area High School in Chester County, Pennsylvania. He has a bachelor's degree in history and a master's degree in education and information systems. Neil is continuing his graduate studies in history at West Chester University. He is the author of *Crimes Against Humanity* in Chelsea House's CRIME, JUSTICE, AND PUNISHMENT series.